DIT; THIS IS!; DOT; THE MIME

A FOUR-SHORT-STORY BOOK

ANGELA K. PAGE

AuthorHouse™
1663 Liberty Drive
Bloomington, IN 47403
www.authorhouse.com
Phone: 1 (800) 839-8640

Published by AuthorHouse 10/09/2018

ISBN: 978-1-5462-6350-0 (sc)
ISBN: 978-1-5462-6351-7 (e)
ISBN: 978-1-5462-6352-4 (hc)

Library of Congress Control Number: 2018912021

Print information available on the last page.

authorHOUSE®

Contents

Dit

By Angela K. Page
Illustrated by Morgan A. Page

Word List

1. A	2. I	3. my	4. am	5. ham	6. an
7. and	8. hand	9. land	10. sand	11. it	12. sit
13. bit	14. pit	15. nit	16. knit	17. mitt	18. cot
19. pot	20. hot	21. bot	22. robot (ro/bot)	23. lot	24. not
25. tot	26. top	27. eat	28. seat	29. feat	30. feet
31.cause	32.gauze	33.because (be/cause)	34.bauble (bau/ble)		

It's Rudimentary
Dit by Angela K. Page

I am Dit!

I am also very fit.

When I do sit for very long,

I play with my mitt.

I also like to look at it.

I eat a little bit.

And, I do not like to hit.

I sit in a pit to hide my big zit!

Because I teach others to knit,

I have a lot of wit.

A. Answer each question in a complete sentence or sentences.

1. Who is the main character in this story? Tell Why.

2. Use the picture to tell what you think being "fit" is.

3. What three-letter word or term do you see in "scary"?

4. Pronounce these 2 words: "us" and "use". Which word has the short "u" sound and which word has the long "u" sound?

5. What are at least 4 actions (verbs) of Dit in the story?

6. Making a comparison: What does Dit not like to do? Are you like Dit? Tell why or why not.

7. What does Dit teach others to do?

8. Pronounce these 2 words: "hid" and "hide". Tell why "hide" has the long "i" sound and "hid" has the short "i" sound?

9. What sound does the "y" make in the words: "my" and "why"?

10. Pronounce these 2 homophones: "not" and "knot".

What are homophones and identify another set from the word list.

11. Identify any term or terms in the word list that you do not know the meaning (s). Find the meaning(s).

12. What sound does "au" make in "cause" and "gauze"?

It Is!

Created by Angela K. Page

Illustrated by Morgan A. Page

Word List

1. A	2. I	3. my	4. me	5. the
6. them	7. this	8. is	9. if	10. in
11.it	12. kit	13. sit	14. no	15. go
16. yes	17. best	18. nest	19.finesse (fi/nesse)	20. ox
21. box	22. fox	23. bike	24. like	25. Mike
26. here	27. there	28. were	29. where	30. wear
31. or	32. nor	33. for	34. bore	35. work
36. four	37. very (ver/y)	38. berry (berr/y)	39. ferry (ferr/y)	40. cherry (cherr/y)

It's Rudimentary
It Is! by Angela K. Page

It is where?

It is here!

No, it's there!

It is an ox.

No, it's a box.

It is a fox.

It is Mike.

Hello there, Mike!

It is a bike.

Yes, it is a bike for Mike!

A. Answer each question in a complete sentence or sentences.

1. What words in the story rhyme with "here", "ox", and "Mike"?

2. What word is the antonym or opposite "No" in the story?

3. Identify a contraction in the story and tell the 2 words it stands for.

4. Use the content and pictures to tell how "here" and "there" are used in the story.

5. List several characters in this story. Tell why you identify them as characters.

6. Identify 2 sets of homophones in the word list.

7. Tell why "bike" and "Mike" have a long "i" sound.

8. How should the statement: "It is where?" be read. Tell why.

Dot

Created by Angela K. Page
Illustrated by Wilma Purcell

Word List

1. is	2. if	3. in	4. fin	5. tin
6. chin	7. skin	8. it	9. sit	10. skit
11. mitt	12. at	13. bat	14. hat	15. that
16. dot	17. cot	18. jot	19. not	20. knot

21. her	22.term	23. better (bet/ter)	24. setter (set/ter)	25. other (oth/er)
26. never (nev/er)	27. come	28. some	29.become (be/come)	30.sometime (some/time)
31. lit	32. little (lit/tle)	33. brittle (brit/tle)	34. settle (set/tle)	35. with
36. pith	37.thither (thith/er)	38. ready (read/y)	39. steady (stead/y)	40.dreadful (dread/ful)
41. us	42. bus	43. thus	44. tusk	45. just

It's Rudimentary
Dot by Angela K. Page
Copyright©2017-2018 by Angela K. Page
All Rights Reserved

I am Dot!

I'm just a little tot.

I work at my desk and
lay on my cot to

jot and play with bots.

**Sometimes, I am not
ready to play**

**on a lot, that has become
very, very hot.**

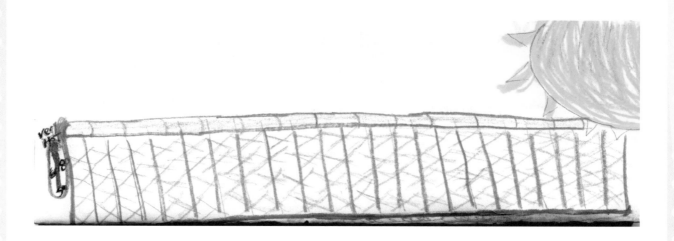

**Thus, I won't play on
the very hot lot.**

A. Answer each question in a complete sentence or sentences.

1. What is the title to this short story? Where is the title of a story found?

2. Characterization: Describe the main character in this story.

3. Use pictures and content to tell your meanings of the following words or terms: "not", "tot", "jot", "cot", "bots", and a "lot".

4. Tell at least two actions (verbs) of Dot in this story.

5. Making a comparison: Are you like Dot? Tell how or how not.

6. Does Dot play on the lot? Tell why or why not.

7. What two words make the contraction: "won't". Tell another contraction in this story. What two words make this contraction?

8. What word is the antonym or opposite of "hot"?

9. How should the statement: "I am Dot!" be read? Tell why.

10. Making an inference: Use content and pictures to tell if you think Dot is "fit" or not.

11. How should this phrase from the story be read: "Thus, I won't play"? Tell why.

12. What sounds do the double vowel "ea" and "y" make in "ready" and "steady"?

The Mime

Created by Angela K. Page

Word List

1. an	2. am	3. my	4. by	5. or
6. nor	7. for	8. form	9. perform (per/form)	10. ask
11. bask	12. task	13. act	14. fact	15. pact
16. to	17. two	18. lime	19. dime	20. time
21. chime	22. mime	23. mine	24. ring	25. during (dur/ing)

It's Rudimentary
The Mime by Angela K. Page
Copyright© 2017-2018 Angela K. Page
All Rights Reserved

I am a mime.

I act with a lime.

I ask for a dime to perform
during my time.

A. Complete each sentence with the correct term based on the story. Answer the questions in a complete sentence or sentences.

1. The main character of the story is a (lime/mime).

2. The character of the story acts with a/an (apple/lime).

3. The character of the story asks for a (dime/nickel).

4. The character of the story performs during his/her (rime/time).

5. From the word list, select a set of homophones.

6. Based on the pictures and content, tell what you think a mime is?

7. Tell why "mime", "chime", and "mine" are read with a long "i" sound.

8. Select 1 term from each question page throughout the book, recite and write the terms in syllables as shown in the word list.

Created at Empowering Learning Institute

The End

Reading Activities

Following are several activities that can be used with this book or any book that the erudite reads. Notice that my children's books are created with a unique format that can easily engage the young reader. First, the children short story is animatedly read to the reader while the young reader points to the word as it is heard. To motivate attentiveness, pause sometimes in the middle of the sentence and allow the young reader to recite the word. Of course, the young reader is expected to respond to the questions following each short story. Some of the responses can be expressed orally, while the others are written in a complete sentence or sentences. To build writing skills, the young erudite is directed to use part of the question in the written response. Knowing your reader, you are encouraged to determine the number of questions and activities that is completed during one setting.

For phonemic awareness activities, the word list can be used to determine how well the young reader recognizes and identifies the sounds of vowels, consonants, and blends. The goal is not to test how well the reader memorizes the spelling of these words. For example, enunciate emphasizing syllables. Provide clues such as "this word has a double vowel with a long vowel sound or a double consonant that is silent." The young reader can pinpoint the phonology of the rhymes; specifically, the identification of the alphabets, blends and the associated sounds.

The young reader can devise a word frequency list, especially indicating the frequency that articles such as "a, an, and the", auxiliary verbs such as "is and are", and other selected words are used. A literary discussion is followed to determine the ability of the young erudite to self discover any syntactical patterns.

With adult assistance, reading rates can be computed. To express the reading rate as the number of words read in 15 or 30 seconds, the young reader records the number of words read while timed. The adult divides the number of words read by .25 or .50 of a minute: the equivalence of 15 or 30 seconds. Imagine how exciting it is for young readers to track reading rates in one second or minute. Just have fun so that the young scholars are motivated to **"Read, Read, and Read!"**

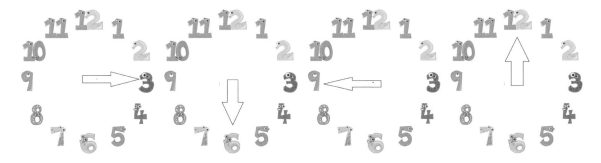

About the Author

Angela Page is a doctoral, hands-on learner and has over 30 years as an educator. Angela is also a Master of Education graduate of Howard University's School of Education in Washington, D.C. She has received many accolades from Outstanding Educator, Women in Science, and Leadership Awards to the Maryland State Presidential Award for Excellence in Mathematics and Science Teaching. After retiring from Prince George's County Public Schools System as a science teacher, she started Empowering Learning Institute. It is an institute where young scholars, scientists, mathematical problem solvers, and junior engineers are nurtured. It is also an institute where Angela receives inspiration to create her children's books. Angela creates these rudimentary reading materials for the novice and for those students who have reading challenges. In her materials, a basic word list is included to practice sounding out and reading words similar to the words in the story. She also encourages vocabulary development through discussion of content clues. Angela Page now lives in Clinton, Maryland with her lovable, supportive family and community.

Printed in the United States
By Bookmasters